Journey
with Jesus
an Easter story

Ann Ingalls   illustrated by Steliyana Doneva

PARACLETE PRESS
BREWSTER, MASSACHUSETTS

Blessed be the God and Father of our Lord Jesus Christ!
By His great mercy He has given us a new birth into a living
hope through the resurrection of Jesus Christ from the dead.
—*1 Peter 1:3, NRSVUE*

For Leonard Hopkins, a fine poet and friend.
—*A.I.*

To the children whom God has given us.
—*S.D.*

2024 First Printing
Journey with Jesus: an Easter Story

Copyright © 2024 by Ann Ingalls

ISBN 978-1-64060-905-1

The Paraclete Press name and logo (dove on cross) are trademarks of Paraclete Press

Library of Congress Control Number: 2023942414

10 9 8 7 6 5 4 3 2 1

Published by Paraclete Press
Brewster, Massachusetts
www.paracletepress.com

Manufactured by RR Donnelley
Printed in Dongguan, China October, 2023

When Jesus rode a peaceful beast,
At Passover, the Jewish feast,
Folks gathered in a joyous swell,
To greet their Lord, Emmanuel.

3

Our Lord and His apostles met
To share a meal they'd not forget.

4

Then Jesus blessed and broke some bread.
He shared a cup of wine and said,
"Keep this forever in your view,
My blood poured out for all of you."

5

Then Jesus got some cloth to cleanse
The dusty feet of His dear friends.
"A new command I give to you:
Love each other as I love you."

That night in dark Gethsemane,
while Jesus prayed in agony,
He was arrested while He prayed.
For silver, Jesus was betrayed.

8

"The one I kiss is who you seek."
Then Judas kissed Him on the cheek.

9

They went to Pilate who accused,
"Who are you then? King of the Jews?"
The trial completed, he decreed
That Jesus walk to Calvary.
"This man is innocent," he sighed.
"Still, take Him to be crucified."

11

Poor Jesus stumbled on His way,
So, Simon bore the cross that day.

His fate a simple cross of wood.
His mother right beneath Him stood.

14

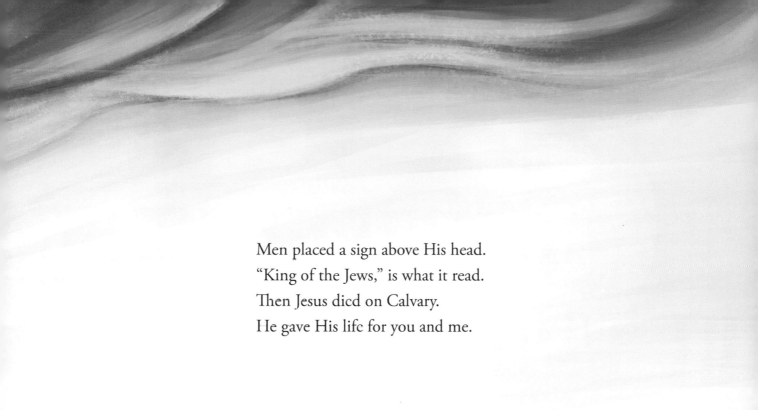

Men placed a sign above His head.
"King of the Jews," is what it read.
Then Jesus died on Calvary.
He gave His life for you and me.

15

And soon the ground began to shake.
The skies grew dark, a huge earthquake!
The guardians were terrified!
"This was the Son of God!" they cried.

Disciples placed Him in a grave,
In Joseph's tomb within a cave.
A heavy stone was rolled in place
At what would be His resting place.

18

But Sunday morning at first light,
Three women saw a wondrous sight!
Those women there were not alone.
An angel rolled away the stone.

"Behold, the Lord whom you revere,
Has risen now. He is not here.
Go look for Jesus, Nazarene.
Tell His disciples what you've seen."

21

The women trembled, yet they went,
To the Upper Room where they were sent,
To where apostles hid from view,
Till Jesus said, "Peace be with you."

He stood among them and beseeched,
"Come see my hands, come see my feet.
I've risen as the Father willed.
What has been written is fulfilled."